Upside Down

A children's book produced by
The Bible Tells Me So Press

PUBLISHED BY
THE BIBLE TELLS ME SO CORPORATION
WWW.THEBIBLETELLSMESO.COM

First Printing, May 2018

Note:

This book is meant to be very interactive.
We hope it will spark many loving, healthy,
and helpful conversations with your child
about some confusing things in the world
around them that might also be...
"upside down."

God's creation
and God's ways
are always perfect!

Sometimes though, people may try to confuse things by rejecting the way God intended them to be. When some people in the Old Testament were doing this, God said through Isaiah,

"You turn things upside down!"

Isaiah 29:16

On the following pages, see if you can tell which things are right, and which things are wrong. Then, turn the book so that the pictures that show how God intended things to be are right side up.

Ready?

Here we go...

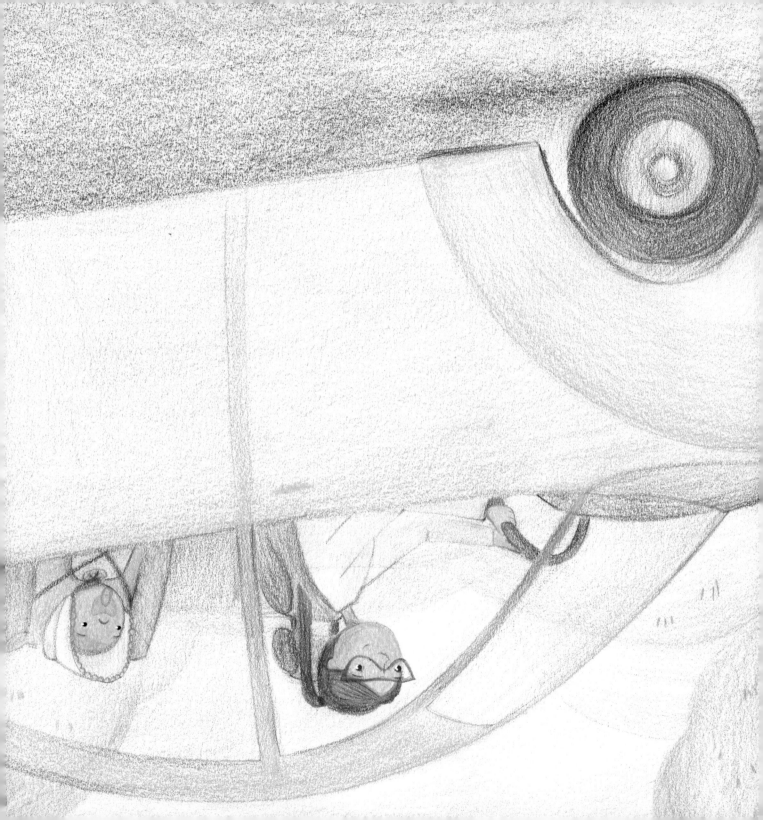

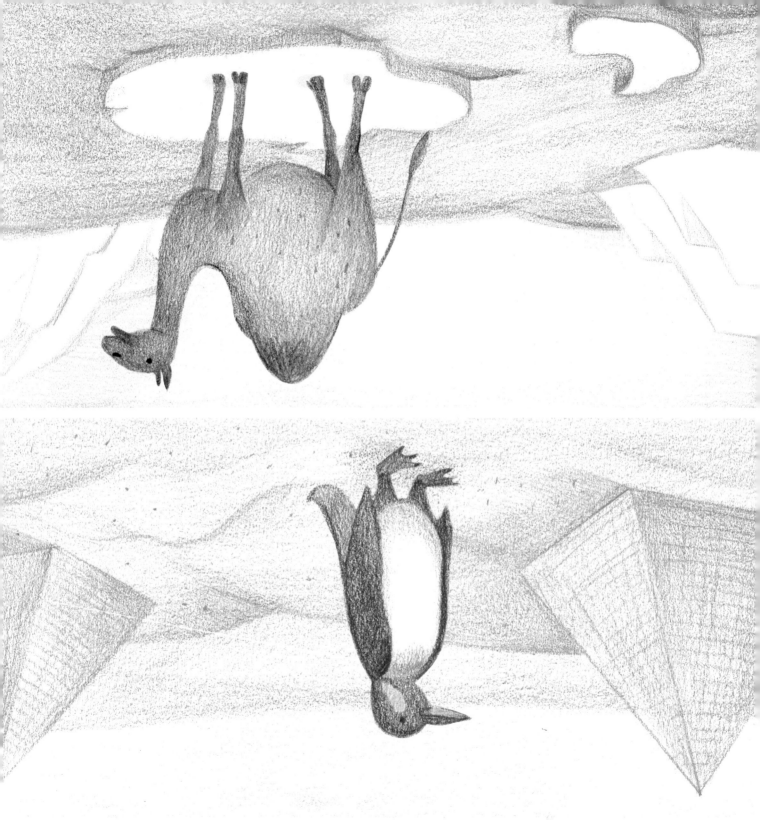

What are some other things you have
seen or heard that are

upside down?

For more
books, videos, songs, and crafts,
visit us online at
TheBibleTellsMeSo.com

Standing on the ~~Rock~~ **and growing!**

Made in the USA
Columbia, SC
05 April 2024

34041612R00015